Everyone loves kittens!

From their adorable whiskery faces and playful paws to their fluffy little tails, kittens are the cutest. Whether snuggled up on your lap, purring contentedly, or chasing after toys, a kitten can be the perfect pet!

There are lots of different types of kittens, each one more adorable than the last: pampered Persians, sleek Siamese, gorgeous Russian Blues or friendly moggies. Open up this diary to find your dream kitten!

All about me

Write all about you, and don't forget
to include some secrets!

Stick your favourite photograph
of yourself here!

My name: saira

My age: 8

My birthday: octobe the 1

My hair colour: blak

My eye colour: brown\blake

My height: 3 Foot 12

Things I love: cooking singing bancing cute animals

Things I hate: being

My favourite food is: Salman

My biggest secret is:

My dream cat would be: white and whith girger pawes

Cat characters

There are lots of breeds of cats, each with their own unique looks and personalities. Here are some of the cutest!

Short-haired

Most pet cats are probably a mixture of short-haired breeds from around the world.

Also known as: moggy
Origin: everywhere!
Eye colour: generally green
Coat: tabby, tortoiseshell, ginger, black, white, mixed colours

Feline fact!
Cats may have been first domesticated over 10,000 years ago – that's a lot of cat lovers!

Siamese

Smart and affectionate, Siamese cats are famous for their loud yowling calls.

Also known as: Moon Diamond
Origin: Thailand (once called Siam)
Eye colour: blue
Coat: white or cream with black, grey or chocolate "points" on the face, feet and tail

Feline fact!
Siamese cats are like dogs – they're super active and love playing fetch with toys!

Persian

These big fluffy cats love catnapping indoors. They're quiet and calm but need a lot of grooming!

Also known as: Longhair
Origin: Iran or Turkey
Eye colour: green, gold or blue
Coat: any colour – tortoiseshell, smokey grey, tabby, white or black.

Feline fact!
Some people clip their Persians' fur to give them manes – like little lions!

Russian Blue

These clever, curious cats make great family pets, but they can be very shy, too.

Also known as: Archangel Blue
Origin: Russia
Eye colour: green
Coat: silvery blue-grey

Feline fact!
Russian Blues are "aristocats" – they might be descended from the Russian tsars' royal cats, and Queen Victoria liked them, too!

Birman

Legend has it that these beautiful animals were originally bred as sacred temple cats.

Also known as: Sacred Cat of Burma
Origin: Burma
Eye colour: blue
Coat: pale cream with darker "points" on the face, legs and tail, and white paws

Feline fact!
Pedigree Birman kittens are given names beginning with a certain letter each year – so kittens born in 2013 all have "K" names!

My perfect kitten profile!

Write all about your perfect kitten. You could describe your real cat, if you have one. If not, just dream up your ideal kitten!

Draw or stick a picture of your perfect kitten here!

Name: LaSma

Breed: birman

Age: 5

Male or female: Female

Coat colour: ginger and white

Eye colour: ~~green~~ terkwous

Favourite toy: yarn

Favourite place to nap: under My
~~in bead~~ bed

Things my kitten loves: yarn frends
coming over

Things my kitten hates: Me going
To frends Milk Riban

Personality: Warm hartid
all wast. ESitid about
some zing

What kitten are you?

If you were a kitten, which breed would you be? This quiz will tell you!

1) My favourite food is...
a) Pasta and muesli – energy for when I'm out and about!
b) Chocolate, and lots of it!
c) Fruit and veggies – they're good for my skin and hair
d) Fish and chips – brain food! ✓

2) My bedroom is...
a) A mess of trainers, balls, racquets and socks.. ✓
b) My special sanctuary, so I keep it nice and neat
c) A pretty haven of beautiful clothes and gorgeous accessories
d) Lined with books and games

3) My favourite kind of film is...
a) Action
b) Comedy
c) Drama ✓
d) Mystery

4) My clothes are...
a) Sleek, sporty and no frills
b) Perfect for lounging about at home ✓
c) The latest trend! ✓
d) Smart but comfortable

5) My favourite time of the year is...
a) Summer – a great time to get out and about
b) Winter – I love snuggling up in a warm, cosy room ✓
c) Spring – time for a wardrobe refresh!
d) Autumn – back to school to see my mates!

6) My ideal birthday party would be...
a) A sports day in the park
b) A sleepover at my house with lots of friends
c) An afternoon out shopping
d) A day trip to a new place ✓

Mostly As...
Spirited Siamese
You're energetic,
always on the go, and
you love playing
sports and games
with your
friends.

Mostly Bs...
Mellow moggy
You're a real housecat
— you love curling up
with a good book and
spending time with
your family.

Mostly Cs...
Pampered Persian
These cats are known
for their good looks,
and you're just as
stylish!

Mostly Ds...
Bright Russian blue
Just like these cats,
you're smart and
curious, and you like to
explore and find out
new things.

Fab cat facts

Be amazed by the wonderful world of cats!

By a whisker

Cats use their whiskers to help them find their way around at night. The long hairs pick up tiny air movements around things, which tell the cat what's up ahead. Whiskers are also handy for measuring a gap to see if it's wide enough to squeeze through!

Rough idea

A cat's cute little rough tongue is covered with tiny hooks made from the same stuff as your fingernails! They allow the cat to give itself a good grooming – it's a little bit like you scratching your head.

Super senses!

Cats have a sense of smell fourteen times better than humans and they can even make out sounds that dogs can't hear! Cats are also great at seeing in the dark – their eyes have a shiny layer which reflects light. Cats are expert hunters – even if all they're tracking are toy mice!

Nine lives

Cats nearly always land on their feet. They can twist their bodies so they are the right way up. Cats can also survive falls from amazing heights, by spreading their bodies to slow their fall. A cat called Andy even lived after falling from the sixteenth floor of his home – but he was very lucky!

Sleep on it

Cats are champions ... at catnapping! Adult cats might snooze for up to twenty hours a day, and will sleep nearly anywhere. This is because cats are hunters, and need to save their energy for catching dinner, even if it is already served up in a bowl!

Old timer

The oldest cat to ever live was Creme Puff, who made it to the amazing age of thirty-eight years! Creme Puff lived in Austin, Texas, USA, and had a very unusual diet of bacon, eggs and broccoli!

Kitten development timeline

In the first few months of their lives, kittens go through a lot of changes. Follow these beautiful Siamese kittens from birth to new homes.

Shh! The newborn kitties are sleeping! They'll stay tucked up with their mum, keeping warm and feeding from her milk for now. They're deaf and blind at this point, and their ears are flattened down.

The kittens have opened their eyes and are strong enough to start crawling around. They even begin to purr for the first time!

Birth	Two weeks	3-4 weeks

Now the kittens are up and about, taking notice of their surroundings. Their ears can hear now, and they've popped up, though they look too big for their heads! The kittens have also got teeth, and their coats are beginning to colour.

Fatty Cats!

These kittens have lots of growing to do. Newborns weigh around 100 grams — that's the same as twenty-five sugar cubes. The kittens feed every hour, and will have doubled in size by the time they're two weeks old!

The mother cat begins to teach her babies how to use the litter tray! They also start to eat solid food. They're very playful and spend more time away from their nest.

The kittens are weaned and house-trained, ready to go to their new homes — and make some mischief!

One month   **Two months**   **Three months**

The kittens are more independent and all their senses are fully developed. They need lots of playtime with people to get used to being pets.

Colour up

Siamese kittens start out all white. Over time, their "points" — the tail, ears, legs and nose — darken. The colouring depends on how warm the cat's body is, which is why it only shows in the coldest parts of their bodies. Siamese cats are paler in warmer countries!

Origami kitten fortune teller

Amaze your friends by predicting what their purr-fect kitten will be like! Use a big piece of square coloured paper, about 20cm by 20cm. Make sure your folds are nice and sharp.

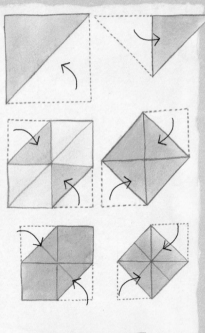

1. Fold your square diagonally in half to make a triangle, and in half again to make a smaller triangle.

2. Open out your paper. Fold in the points to the centre to form a smaller square.

3. Now flip over your smaller square and fold in the points to the centre, so you have an even smaller square!

4. Fold the square in half to make a rectangle, and unfold. Then crease the square in half the other way, before unfolding again.

5. To pull the fortune teller into shape, push the four corners together, and place the thumb and index finger of each hand inside the flaps on the underside.

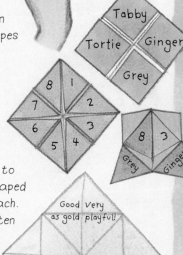

6. Now to write the fortunes. On the outside flaps, write four types of cat coat colour, e.g. Tabby, Ginger, Tortoiseshell and Grey.

7. On the flaps facing inwards, number the triangular folds from 1 to 8.

8. Open out the numbered flaps to reveal another four diamond-shaped flaps. Write two fortunes on each. Fortunes could include "Your kitten will be good as gold," or "Your kitten will be extra playful!"

How to play:

Fold your fortune teller back up as shown in step 5. Insert your thumbs and fingers inside each of the four flaps. Ask a friend to pick her favourite coat colour. Then spell out the colour she chooses, closing and opening the teller top to bottom, then side to side, for each letter.

Stop on the last letter and ask her to pick one of the numbers she can see. Count up to her number, closing and opening the teller as before.

When you finish, ask her to pick another number from the four flaps shown. Open the flap to predict her ideal kitten!

Fictional Felines

These memorable moggies are the stars
of film, stage and books!

Crookshanks

Crookshanks is the tatty pet
of Hermione Granger in the
Harry Potter books by J K
Rowling. Described as big, ginger
and bandy-legged, Crookshanks is
actually half "kneazle", an
intelligent magical species in the
books. In the films, he is played
by a Persian called
Crackerjack.

The Aristocats

The Aristocats is an animation
about a pampered cat family who
are forced to fend for themselves
on the streets of Paris. The mother
cat Duchess and her three kittens
are helped by a streetwise alley
cat called Thomas. Its best-known
song is "Ev'rybody Wants To Be
A Cat", by Scat Cat and
his jazz band.

The Owl and
the Pussycat

Edward Lear wrote this
much-loved nonsense poem in the
nineteenth century. It follows the
cat and the owl as they sail
off in a "beautiful pea-green
boat". They are married by
a turkey, and use a ring
from a pig's nose!

Cats!

This musical by Andrew Lloyd Webber was inspired by T S Eliot's poetry book Old Possum's Book of Practical Cats. The much-loved characters include Macavity the cat burglar, and the magical Mr Mistoffelees. It's famous for Grizabella, the faded glamour cat, and her wistful song, "Memory".

The Cheshire Cat

This cool cat features in Lewis Carroll's classic story Alice in Wonderland. He confuses Alice by disappearing into thin air, leaving only his wide toothy grin. He later outwits the Queen of Hearts by making just his head appear!

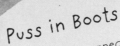

Puss in Boots

Puss in Boots has appeared in everything from pantomimes to films. He was created by French author Charles Perrault in 1697. His story sees a poor miller's son inherit a talking cat who insists on wearing a pair of boots. The loyal cat tricks a king and outsmarts an ogre, before finally winning the young man's fortune.

How to draw a cat

Learn how to draw your favourite pet in six simple steps. Make it your own with colour and markings.

Step 1
Using a soft pencil, draw a round circle for the kitten's head and an oval shape for its body.

step 2
Add two triangles for its ears and draw in the cheeks. Draw a faint horizontal line halfway down the face.

Step 3
Draw in lines for the front legs and a curve for the back leg. Add in a curve for the tail. Join up the two circles with lines for the neck.

Step 4
Now you can sketch in
more of the detail.
Draw in the eyes on the
line. Add a triangular
nose and a mouth.
Join up the bridge of
the nose with the eyes.

Step 5
Rub out the horizontal line
and the bottom of the oval
shape. Add in the paws and
draw in another curve to
complete the tail.

Step 6
Add in the last
details using light
pencil marks for the
fur. You can also
colour it in with
your favourite cat
markings. Here is a
ginger tabby!

Cat Wordsearch

Using the clues below, find the missing cat words in the puzzle! Words could run across, down or diagonally.

1. Puss in _boots_ is a famous fictional cat who you can see at the panto.

2. If a cat hisses, she's angry! You should watch out for her teeth and _claws_!

3. A cat wears a _collar_ with a label so he can be returned home if he gets lost.

4. A cat might cough up a _perball_. Gross!

5. A baby cat is called a _kitten_.

6. Cats are said to have nine _lives_.

7. A cat will _meow_ when she wants attention!

8. The _persion_ is a breed of cat with lots of fluffy fur.

9. When a cat is happy, he will _perr_.

10. You should never give a cat milk, instead just give him _water_.

r	r	x	c	l	a	w	s	v	u
f	k	a	r	b	o	o	t	s	m
u	p	c	e	c	l	m	r	t	r
r	e	w	q	p	u	r	r	e	g
b	r	t	u	h	s	p	t	b	o
a	s	c	o	l	l	a	r	m	d
l	i	w	g	o	w	q	g	e	i
l	a	k	i	t	t	e	n	o	o
s	n	t	u	n	g	g	n	w	t
j	e	i	l	i	v	e	s	f	w

ANSWERS!

1. Boots   6. lives
2. claws   7. meow
3. collar   8. Persian
4. furball   9. purr
5. kitten   10. water

Gingerbread kittens

These scrummy cat-shaped gingerbread
biscuits are easy to make and fun to decorate!

Ingredients:
- 175g flour, plus more
for dusting
- 90g soft light brown
sugar
- 1 teaspoon each of
ground ginger, mixed
spice and ground
cinnamon
- 1 teaspoon bicarbonate
of soda
- 60g butter, softened
and cubed
- 1 small egg
- 2 tablespoons golden
syrup
- writing icing
- sweets or sugar
silver balls

You will need:
- mixing bowl
- teaspoons
- wooden spoon or electric
whisk
- cling film
- rolling pin
- cookie cutter, 8cm diameter
- knife
- baking trays
- greaseproof paper
- wire cooling rack
- an adult to help you!

Makes about 10 biscuits

What to do:

1. Put the flour, sugar, spices and bicarbonate of soda in the bowl and mix in the butter. The mixture will look like breadcrumbs.

2. Beat in the egg and golden syrup until the mixture forms a soft, light brown dough. Roll into a ball and wrap in cling film, before putting in the fridge for 15 minutes.

3. Heat the oven to 180°C/350°F and line the trays with greaseproof paper.

4. Lay cling film on to your kitchen surface, flour it, and place the chilled dough on it. Dust the rolling pin with flour, and roll out the dough to a 5mm thickness.

5. Using the cookie cutter, cut out a circle of dough. Carefully peel it off the cling film and place it on a tray. Cut out two small triangles and arrange them at the top of the circle like a cat's ears. Repeat until all the dough is used up, spacing out the biscuits.

6. Place the trays in the oven and bake for 12-15 minutes. The biscuits should be golden brown when you take them out. Leave them for 15 minutes, before putting the biscuits on a wire rack to cool and harden.

7. Now you can decorate! Draw a face using the writing icing and stick sweets to the biscuit for the eyes and nose.

YUM!

Mythic moggies

People have loved cats for a long time,
and even worshipped them!

Cat gods

Cats and lions were sacred to the
ancient Egyptians. They worshipped
the cat-headed goddess Bastet,
daughter of the great sun god Ra.
Bastet used her reflective eyes to guard
Ra during the night, ensuring the sun rose
again. The Egyptians loved their pet cats
too, and when one died, it would be
mummified so it could pass into the
afterlife. The owner would even
shave off his eyebrows in
mourning!

Cat chariot

The Norse people of Scandinavia
believed in the gods Thor and
Freyja, amongst others. Freyja
was the beautiful goddess of
love and magic. She travelled in
a chariot drawn by two
enormous grey cats called
Bygul and Trjegul, that Thor
had given to her.

Black magic

In medieval Europe people thought that black cats were "familiars" – animals that the devil had sent to help witches work their dark magic... But the superstition didn't last – in Britain, a black cat crossing your path is said to bring good fortune, and sailors used to think a black ship's cat was especially lucky.

Maneki-neko

Once upon a time in Japan, a rich lord passed by a cat sitting at a temple entrance. It beckoned to him with its paw. Curious, he followed the cat inside, only to hear a clap of thunder – lightning had struck the very spot where he had just been standing! The lord was amazed and donated lots of money to the poor temple. Nowadays, oriental shops often have a Maneki-neko, or "waving cat" figurine to bring good luck.

Let sleeping cats lie

In Islamic countries, cats are the preferred pets. One legend tells of the Prophet Muhammad finding a cat sleeping on the sleeve of his coat. He needed to wear the coat to prayer, but rather than disturb the cat, he cut off the sleeve!

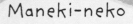

Fact or fiction?

Can you tell the totally true facts from the fishy falsehoods?

1. When you move house, rub butter on your cat's paws to stop it from getting lost looking for its old home.

2. Ginger cats are usually boys.

3. Bells on collars help stop cats from hunting garden birds.

4. Cats should have plenty of cow's milk.

5. Cats have nine lives.

6. Cats mustn't eat dog food, but dogs can sometimes eat cat food!

7. Cats only purr when they are happy.

8. All cats hate water.

9. Cats use their tails for balance.

Now flip for the answers!

1. False. People used to think rubbing butter on a cat's paws would make it clean itself in the new home, giving it time to settle in. Instead, keep your cat indoors for two weeks, and make sure it's microchipped.

2. True. Gingers are usually tomcats. But it is possible to have a girl ginger kitten.

3. False. The only way to stop a cat from hunting is to keep it inside. Although jingling bells may scare off the prey, cats can learn to move so stealthily that their bells don't ring!

4. False. Cow's milk makes cats sick – they cannot digest the sugar in it. Kittens can have special milk for cats, but when they grow up, they just need water.

5. False. This myth probably came from a time when people believed black cats were magical demons in disguise!

6. True. Dog food doesn't have enough meat in it to keep cats healthy. But it won't harm your dog if it steals the cat's food once in a while – unless the cat finds out!

7. False. Cats do purr when they're happy, but they sometimes purr when they're in pain, too.

8. False. There is a breed of cat called the Turkish Van. These cats love to swim and catch fish!

9. True. Cats use their tails as a counterweight, especially when climbing trees.

Sock mouse toy

Make a mouse toy for your kitten to play with — if you haven't got a cat, you could donate this toy to the local cat shelter!

You will need:
- sock
- marker pen
- a small piece of felt
- non-toxic fabric glue
- cotton stuffing
- catnip, available from pet shops
- ribbon
- scissors
- an adult to help you!

1. Cut off the top piece of the sock at the ankle. The foot part of the sock will be the mouse's body — turn it over so the sock's sole is facing up.

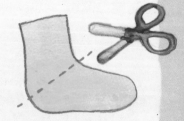

2. Stuff your mouse with the cotton stuffing, so that it is full and squishy, and a bit fatter at the heel end. Add some catnip to make it even more fun for your kitty!

3. Glue the ribbon into the stuffing at the opening.

4. Gather the sock together at the opening so it is taut and glue together. Ensure that the ribbon is firmly stuck in place.

5. Draw the eyes of the mouse near the toe end with the marker pen.

6. Take your piece of felt and cut out a triangle for a nose. Glue it on to the sock's toe end.

7. For the ears, cut two circles from the felt. Put a blob of glue near the edge of each circle. Pinch the circle together on either side of the glue and leave to dry. Then glue the ears on to the mouse's head. Leave to dry completely. Now you have a toy to keep your kitten entertained!

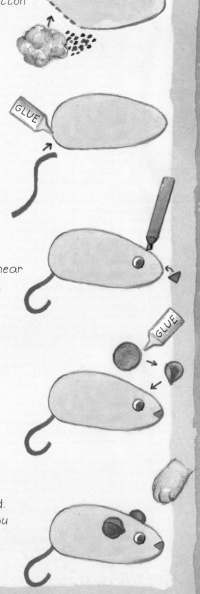

The perfect kitten space

Kittens need lots of things to keep them happy and healthy. Here's what to put in your new kitten's purr-fect home!

Cat flap
This is the kitten's front door! She must wait until she's had all her vaccinations before she can go out and play.

Scratching post
The kitten loves to sharpen her claws on this post, and there is a dangly toy to play with too!

Litter tray
Lined with fresh litter. There are also some old newspapers underneath in case there are any accidents!

Food and water bowls
These are shallow so she can get at her food and fresh water.

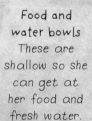

Window ledge
Cats love to climb
on to ledges and
watch the world
go by.

Boxes
These are a
simple and fun
playhouse for
your kitten.
Cut holes in the
boxes so she
can play hide
and seek!

Brush
Long-furred cats
need a good brush
each day.

Toys
Hours of fun can be
had playing with your
kitten and her toys!

Cat bed
With a big fluffy
cushion and soft
blanket to make it
extra cosy.

What am I thinking?

Cats use body language to show how they're feeling. Match the thoughts to the kittens!

1. There's a big scary dog in my house! Go away!

2 I'm hungry! I'd better ask my owner for a snack.

3. I don't know what this fluffy thing is, but I love playtime!

4. I'm ready for my tummy tickle!

5. Ready ... steady ... POUNCE!

6. I've been out and about, and now I need a good wash!

7. Play with me, now, please!

8. What's that noise? It's woken me up!

9. Puuurrr! This is such a comfortable spot!

10. Hello! I'm happy to see you!

11. I think I might be a bit stuck, now!

12. No one will ever find me here!

A   B   C   D   E   F   G   H   I   J   K   L

ANSWERS:
1G, 2D, 3E, 4I, 5A, 6F, 7H, 8J, 9L, 10B, 11C, 12K

The Greenhouse Kitten

By Holly Webb

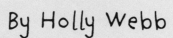

"Sophie, can you pick me some tomatoes out of the greenhouse?"

Sophie looked up from the little vegetable patch where she was weeding around her pumpkin plant. It had four baby pumpkins on it. She wanted at least one of them to get big enough to make a lantern for Halloween. It seemed a long time until then, but they were still only the size of satsumas, so there was still a way to go.

Sophie went to the kitchen window. "How many should I pick?"

Her mum held out a bowl. "Just a few to have in a salad for lunch. Thanks!"

Sophie ran down to the greenhouse. It was a really hot day, and Mum had told her to leave the door open after they'd watered the plants early that morning. She gasped – it was steaming hot inside, even with the door open. The warmth wrapped itself round Sophie like a damp blanket. It was like a tiny patch of thick jungle in their garden. The tomato plants were huge, even taller than Sophie, some of them. She loved picking tomatoes, searching under the hairy green leaves for the glowing red fruit. There were lots today – it had been so hot, they were all ripening up, scarlet and glossy.

Sophie crouched down to get at a particularly juicy-looking tomato, and gasped again. Staring out at her between the leaves was a small, furry face.

The Greenhouse Kitten

Sophie was so surprised that she nearly fell over. Whatever it was that was hiding behind the tomato plants seemed to be surprised, too. The little face disappeared, and there was a scuffling noise and a shaking of leaves as the creature darted away into the furthest corner of the greenhouse.

Sophie sat back on her heels and stared after it. She had only had the tiniest glimpse, but she was sure – almost sure – that it had been a kitten. There had been round, bright green eyes, a little pinkish-brown nose, and a great moustache of white whiskers. What on earth was a kitten doing in their greenhouse?

Who did it belong to? Sophie was pretty sure that none of their neighbours even had a cat. She would have noticed. She knew every cat on the way to school, and their owners. She loved all the cats so much that Mum and Dad had told her that maybe they could have one of their own some day. But they hadn't said when.

As Sophie watched, the tips of those white whiskers shimmered out from between the tomato leaves. Sophie squeezed her fingers together excitedly. She had sat still enough! The kitten was coming out!

Very slowly, the rest of the whiskers appeared, and then the tips of two reddish-brown ears, with the tiniest little furry tufts on them, like a wildcat.

The Greenhouse Kitten

Sophie and the kitten stared at each other silently. Then the kitten shook itself a little (Sophie could tell, because the tomato plants shook too) and padded delicately out into the middle of the greenhouse.

He was possibly the prettiest kitten Sophie had ever seen. He was mostly ginger, with a white chest and the greenest eyes. Even greener than Alfie, her gran's cat. Sophie went round to Gran's every Thursday after school, and Gran said that Alfie was a little bit Sophie's too. He adored her, and she always brought him cat treats.

The kitten stepped closer, his whiskers twitching with curiosity. Sophie was just about managing to keep still, even though her feet were going to sleep, and her heart was thumping with excitement. She had a feeling he was a boy kitten – he had big ears, and big paws (fat orange stripy ones) and he looked like he was going to grow up into a big cat. But his body was very skinny, and Sophie wondered if he was a stray, and how long he'd been away from his mother.

What she really wanted to do was reach out and pick the kitten up, but she didn't want to scare him away. He might shoot back out the door of the greenhouse, and she'd never see him again.

"Sophie! What's happened to those tomatoes?"

Sophie and the kitten froze. She saw his shoulders hunch up nervously, and she dug her fingernails into her palms, hoping that he wouldn't run away.

Sophie's mum had walked up to the greenhouse door. Sophie turned her head, very slowly, putting her finger to her lips, and giving her mum a desperate "don't scare him" look.

"A kitten…" her mum whispered. "Oh my goodness." She stood quietly in the doorway, staring at the visitor.

"He was hiding behind the tomato plants," Sophie whispered back, watching the kitten's ears twitching nervously back and forth as he listened to them. She flicked a hopeful sideways glance at her mum. "He looks hungry."

Her mum frowned a little. "I suppose he does. But I'm not sure we should feed him, Sophie. He might belong to someone. We'd be stopping him going home."

The kitten took a cautious step forward, and stretched his thin neck out to sniff at Sophie's hands. His whiskers tickled, and she tried not to giggle.

"I don't think he does belong to anyone," Sophie whispered. "He's so thin, look. And he doesn't have a collar. He's a stray, I'm sure he is." Very gently, she reached out one hand – her fingers felt stiff, she'd been keeping still for so long – and stroked the top of his head.

The kitten darted back a little, and then he seemed to realize that Sophie meant to be nice, and he butted his head into the palm of her hand. His fur was incredibly soft, and his huge ears were silky.

"Oh… He's lovely," Sophie whispered.

"I suppose it would be all right to give him a little bit of left-over chicken," Mum said. "He *is* beautiful. The chicken was going to be your lunch…"

"I don't mind!" Sophie said quickly.

"Mum, if he's a stray – could we keep him? You did say maybe we could have our own cat one day, and this kitten's come and found us. It's like he wants to be ours."

"I don't know, Sophie." Mum shook her head. "He must belong to somebody. What if we start thinking he's ours, and then we have to give him back to his real owner? It would be so sad."

"I suppose so." Sophie sighed. "But what are we going to do with him? How do we find out where he belongs? Oh! Maybe he's got a microchip, like Alfie! We could take him to the vet to check."

"Yes, maybe. And even if he hasn't, the vet could tell us what we should do. I wonder if we could tempt him into a box with some chicken?" Mum said thoughtfully. "I'll go and find one."

The Greenhouse Kitten

Sophie watched sadly as Mum went back to the house. "I wish you'd disappear, just for a little while, so we wouldn't be able to take you to the vet," she told the kitten. He was nosing at her fingers now, his front paws up on her knee. "I don't want to find your owners at all. But I suppose they're missing you."

The kitten looked up at her as she crouched, and then sprang into her lap, purring a little.

Sophie gaped at him. She hadn't expected him to do that at all. "Oh, you're so friendly. You're gorgeous," she told him, stroking him very gently down his back. She wriggled herself into a sitting position, so she could cuddle him properly, and the kitten snuggled happily into her arms.

Sophie was enjoying stroking the kitten so much that she had hardly noticed her mother was away for much longer than it would take to find a box. Sophie didn't even hear the phone ringing, she was too busy crooning compliments to the kitten, and listening to his deep, throaty purr.

But eventually her mother came back up the path with a saucer of cold chicken, and Sophie noticed that she looked quite stunned. "What's the matter?" she asked. "Couldn't you find a box?"

"I didn't look… That was your gran on the phone," said her mum, placing the saucer on the floor. The kitten took a flying leap off Sophie's lap, and began to wolf down the chicken.

The Greenhouse Kitten

Sophie giggled. "He looks as though he hasn't eaten for days!"

Her mum nodded. "He might not have done. He's been gone for five days, apparently."

Sophie stared at Mum. "How do you know?"

Mum smiled. "Gran told me! She always knows everything. This kitten belongs to a lady in Gran's reading group, who lives down the end of her road. Her cat had kittens, and a ginger one escaped out of the front door when she went out to pick up her milk. She's quite elderly, and she couldn't catch him. She left food out, and put up notices, but he didn't come back. She was telling Gran all about it at reading group last night. Gran was ringing to say keep an eye out for him!

She thought you might spot him, the way you know all the cats round here." Mum chuckled. "She was quite surprised when I told her you'd already found him… It has to be him, surely?"

"Yes." Sophie smiled down at the kitten, but her eyes were full of tears. "I suppose we ought to go and give him back. Can he finish the chicken first?" She sniffed.

Mum crouched down next to her. "He can. And then maybe we ought to buy him some cat food. He must be starving."

Sophie frowned at her. "What do you mean? Won't his owner have food?"

"I'm sure she does. But your gran's ringing her up right now, to say we've found the kitten, and that we'd like to keep him. She needed to find homes for all of her kittens anyway, Sophie. And like you said – he found us."

"Really?" Sophie felt like bouncing up and hugging her mum, but she didn't want to scare the kitten. He had finished the chicken now, and was climbing back in to her lap. It took a bit of effort – his tummy was a lot rounder than it had been before.

"Really. Look, I've brought my mobile – do you want to call Dad and see what he thinks?"

Sophie nodded, but she looked worried. "Do you reckon he'll say yes?"

Mum smiled. "He might be a bit surprised. But I think so." She handed Sophie the phone, and Sophie listened anxiously to it ringing. The kitten twitched his ears curiously at the noise.

"Dad! I'm in the greenhouse, and I've found a kitten in the tomato plants, and the lady who lost him wants to find a home for him, so can we keep him, pleeeease?"

There was silence for a moment on the other end of the line, and then Dad said, "Run that past me again, Soph?"

"He's a lost kitten. But Gran knows who he belongs to, and he needs a home."

"In the greenhouse?" Dad still sounded confused.

"No! With us, silly." Sophie giggled. She could tell from Dad's voice that he was going to say yes.

"And Mum says we can have him?"

Sophie looked at her mum, and held the phone out, her eyes pleading.

Mum spoke to Dad. "He is gorgeous. And it seems like we're meant to have him. I know it's sooner than we planned … mm-hm." She smiled down at Sophie. "Dad says you'd better call him Tom."

"So we can keep him?" Sophie gave a shaky little sigh of relief. "But why Tom?" She looked down at the kitten, stretched out and purring on her lap.

Her mum grinned at her. "Short for tomato."

Sophie rolled her eyes. "Trust Dad."

Mum tickled the purring kitten under the chin. "Why don't you see if he's happy to come inside?"

Sophie gently slipped her hands around Tom the kitten, and cradled him against her shoulder. And then she carried him down the path, to go and see his new home.

Secret kitten diary

This secret diary is just for you.
Fill in your friends' birthdays,
family celebrations and holidays, too.

Year of diary:

.............2013/14.............

This diary belongs to:

Saira

Address:

███████████

███████████

Telephone:

Email:

Birthday:

███████████

January

1	2	3	4
5	6	7	8
9	10	11	12
13	14	15 *Love more birthday*	16

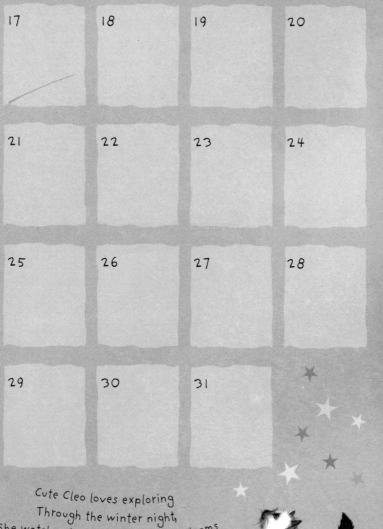

17	18	19	20
21	22	23	24
25	26	27	28
29	30	31	

Cute Cleo loves exploring
Through the winter night,
She watches how the white moon gleams
And all the stars shine bright!

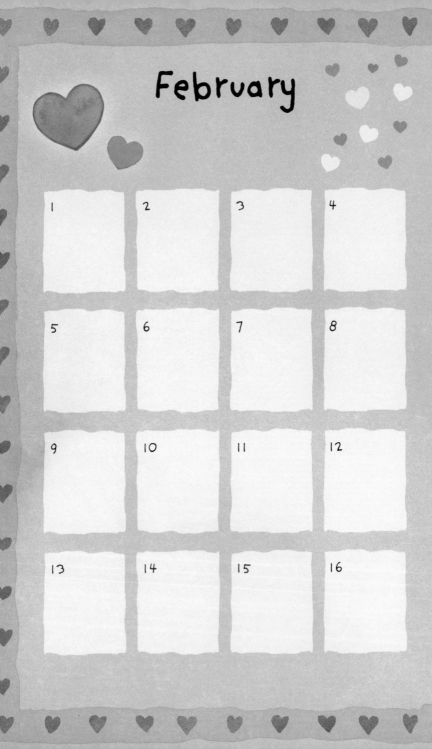

February

1	2	3	4
5	6	7	8
9	10	11	12
13	14	15	16

17

18

Mom's
birthday

19

20

21

22

23

24

25

26

27

28

(29)

Pretty Ginger's very shy
But he will sometimes purr.
He loves it if you scratch his ears
And stroke his short soft fur!

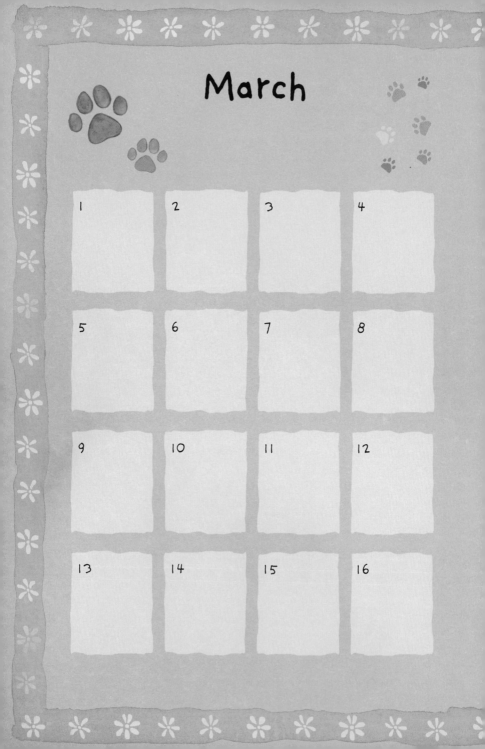

17	18	19	20
21	22	23	24
25	26	27	28
29	30	31	

Fluff is learning tricks and games
And though he's really small
He loves to run across the floor
To chase his special ball!

April

1	2	3	4
5	6	7	8 ~~Tanya's~~
9	10	11	12
13	14	15	16

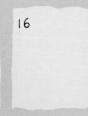

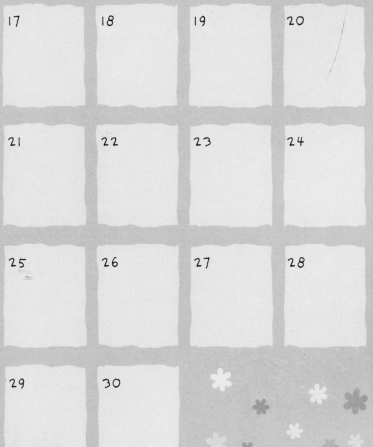

17   18   19   20

21   22   23   24

25   26   27   28

29   30

When the garden's green and lush
And spring is in the air,
Kitty loves to scamper round
Exploring everywhere!

May

1	2	3	4
5	6	7	8
9	10	11	12
13	14	15	16

17	18	19	20
21	22	23	24
25	26	27	28
29	30	31	

In the field of buttercups
Whiskers jumps about
She crouches in the long green grass
Then quickly pounces out!

June

1	2	3	4
5	6	7	8
9	10	11	12
13	14	15	16

17

18

19

20

21

22

23

24

25

26

27

28

29

30

What a lovely summer's day!
The sky is clear and blue
And Patch is waiting patiently
To say meow to you!

July

1	2	3	4
5	6	7	8
9	10	11	12
13	14	15	16

17

18

19

20

21

22

23

24

25

26

27

28

29

30

31

Misty loves to bounce and play
Exploring everywhere
Chasing string and balls of wool
Running here and there!

August

1	2	3	4
5	6	7	8 Talyas birt bay
9	10	11	12
13	14	15	16

17	18	19	20
21	22	23	24
25	26	27	28
29	30	31	

Max is always out and about
He's good at climbing trees,
He'll find a spot to stretch out
And enjoy the summer breeze!

September

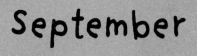

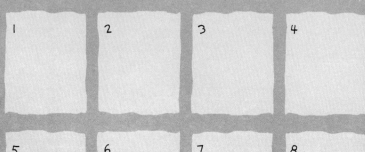

1	2	3	4
5	6	7	8
9	10	11	12
13	14	15	16

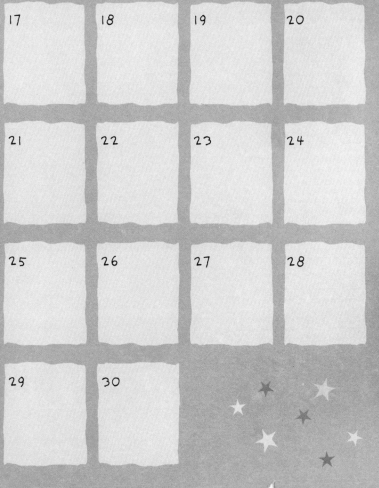

17

18

19

20

21

22

23

24

25

26

27

28

29

30

The evening sky turns purple
It's such a lovely sight!
And Sheba's heading home for tea
As day turns into night!

October

1 My birthday	2	3	4
5	6	7	8
9	10	11	12
13	14	15	16

17	18	19	20
21	22	23	24
25	26	27	28
29	30	31	

Socks likes playing in the leaves.
She loves the crunching sound!
She whisks her tail to and fro
and pounces round and round!

November

1

2

3

4

5

6

7

8

9

10

11

12

13

14

15

16

17 18 19 20

21 22 23 24

25 26 27 28

29 30

As the wind comes whistlng by
And snow falls to the ground,
Pepper sits and watches how
The flakes spin round and round!

December

1	2	3	4
5	6	7	8
9	10	11	12
13	14	15	16